Bridges

{IT CHANGED THE WORLD}

INVENTION OF
PHONES

Jennifer Reed

A Division of
Carson Dellosa Education

rourkeeducationalmedia.com

Before Reading: *Building Background Knowledge and Vocabulary*

Building background knowledge can help children process new information and build upon what they already know. Before reading a book, it is important to tap into what children already know about the topic. This will help them develop their vocabulary and increase their reading comprehension.

Questions and Activities to Build Background Knowledge:

1. Look at the front cover of the book and read the title. What do you think this book will be about?
2. What do you already know about this topic?
3. Take a book walk and skim the pages. Look at the table of contents, photographs, captions, and bold words. Did these text features give you any information or predictions about what you will read in this book?

Vocabulary: *Vocabulary Is Key to Reading Comprehension*

Use the following directions to prompt a conversation about each word.

- Read the vocabulary words.
- What comes to mind when you see each word?
- What do you think each word means?

> **Vocabulary Words:**
> - economy
> - networks
> - patent office
> - production
> - pulses
> - receiver
> - satellite
> - switchboard
> - telegraphs
> - transmitted

During Reading: *Reading for Meaning and Understanding*

To achieve deep comprehension of a book, children are encouraged to use close reading strategies. During reading, it is important to have children stop and make connections. These connections result in deeper analysis and understanding of a book.

 ### Close Reading a Text

During reading, have children stop and talk about the following:

- Any confusing parts
- Any unknown words
- Text to text, text to self, text to world connections
- The main idea in each chapter or heading

Encourage children to use context clues to determine the meaning of any unknown words. These strategies will help children learn to analyze the text more thoroughly as they read.

When you are finished reading this book, turn to the next-to-last page for **Text-Dependent Questions** and an **Extension Activity**.

TABLE OF CONTENTS

COMMUNICATION BEFORE THE PHONE

How would you talk to a friend in another neighborhood if you didn't have a telephone or computer? Before either of these things was invented, getting a message to someone was hard. If the message had to travel long distances, it could take weeks or months depending on how far away someone lived.

Some messages could be sent over short distances using flags, fire, or lights as codes. The smoke signal is one of the oldest forms of long-distance communication.

MAIL BY PONY

The Pony Express was a mail service that started operations in 1860. It used a system of horses and riders to deliver messages, newspapers, and mail. The route ran about 2,000 miles (3,219 kilometers) from Missouri to California. Sending mail through the full route took about ten days.

A breakthrough in long-distance communication came with the invention of Morse code. It was a system of dots and dashes that was often used with electric **telegraphs**. This technology **transmitted** coded messages through wires as electrical **pulses** that made beeping noises on the receiving end.

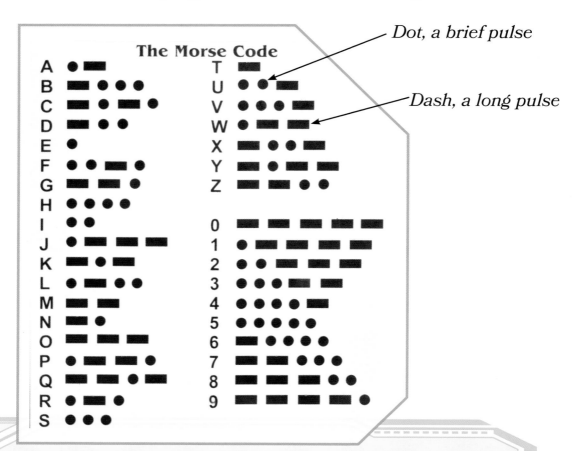

Dot, a brief pulse

Dash, a long pulse

THE FIRST TELEGRAPH MESSAGE

Samuel Morse sent the first officially recognized telegraph message on May 24, 1844. It went across a wire that stretched 40 miles (about 64 kilometers) from Washington, D.C. to Baltimore, Maryland. The message said, "What hath God wrought?" It took just a few seconds to transmit.

TELEGRAPH TO TELEPHONE

Think about what it would be like to wait hours or even days to get a response to a message. The telegraph changed that for individuals, businesses, newspapers, and the military. Communication between countries expanded when a telegraph wire was laid across the Atlantic Ocean to Europe.

Messages needing a quick reply could be sent and received in a short amount of time, often seconds or minutes. Telegraphs could also be used to direct the transfer of money from one account to another. At first, only one message could be sent on the wire at a time. Later, an invention allowed four connections on a single line, so four messages could be sent at once.

The first telegraph cable across the Atlantic Ocean was laid in 1865. The map shows the long-distance cables that came later.

WESTERN UNION
RANS-ATLANTIC CABLES
AND CONNECTIONS

Reykiavik

Faroe Is.

Shetland Is.

Bergen

Orkney Is.

Ekersund

Aberdeen

SCOTLAND

BRITISH ISLES   Edinburgh DENM

Newcastle

IRELAND   ENGLAND

Dublin   Liverpool

Valentia   Lowestoft

London

NEWFOUNBLAND   Bristol

Antwerp

Harbor Grace   Bru

tent   Penzance   BEL

Placentia   Havre

St. Pierre   Bresto   Paris

A T L A N T I C   FRANCE

Marseille

Bilbao

Algiers

O   C   Golea

 pe

ue   FRI

los

Soko

rgetown   NIG

Paramaribo

ANA   Cayenne

The telegraph soon gave way to the invention of the telephone. Telephones turn your voice into an electrical signal that can travel through wires to a **receiver**, where a listener can hear it.

No one is sure who invented the first telephone because many inventors were trying at once. Alexander Graham Bell and Elisha Gray were two such inventors. In 1876, they raced to be the first to register a telephone device with the **patent office** in Washington, D.C. Bell beat Gray by just a few hours.

Elisha Gray's telephone design used water to carry signals.

BELL'S FIRST TELEPHONE 1875

10. **First Bell Telephone**
June 1875

Bell's new device transmitted voices through a wire. The first message he sent was to his assistant, Thomas Watson: "Mr. Watson, come here; I want to see you." Watson was at the receiving end of the machine in another room and clearly heard every word.

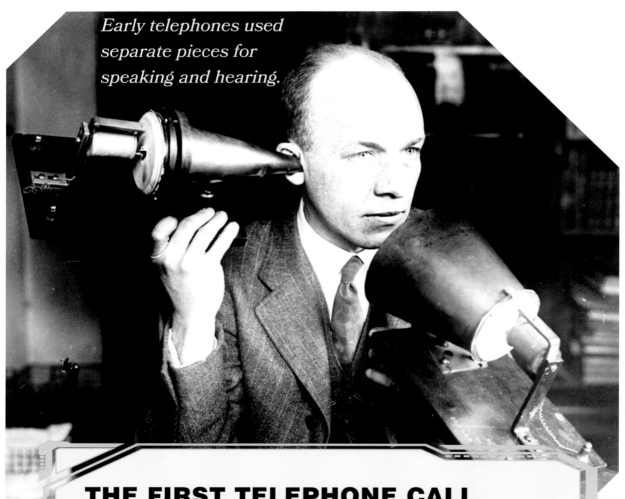

Early telephones used separate pieces for speaking and hearing.

THE FIRST TELEPHONE CALL

On October 9, 1876, Bell and Watson talked by telephone between Cambridge and Boston, Massachusetts. They were two miles (about 3.2 kilometers) apart. It was the first reported voice conversation ever held over wire.

When Alexander Graham Bell helped open a long-distance phone line from New York City, New York, to Chicago, Illinois, many people wanted to see it work for themselves.

A NEW WORLD

At first, mostly businesses used telephones, which were so expensive that many individuals could not afford them. Electric lines were a new invention at this time, and they changed how people lived and businesses worked. Businesses didn't have to wait for an order to be mailed in. They could take orders, talk with customers, and increase **production** through the telephone.

As businesses grew, they created new jobs. Communities were created around the businesses. People moved from rural areas to cities as a result. The new telephone **networks** made the growth of urban areas possible.

By 1885, cities were full of telephone and electric lines.

By 1918, technology and jobs had improved so much that about ten million Bell telephones were in service in the United States. The telephone helped save lives by making it easier and faster to talk with a doctor or call the fire or police departments.

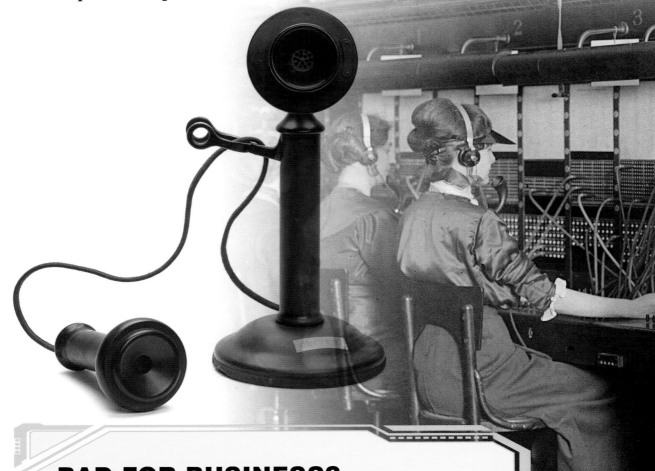

BAD FOR BUSINESS?

Telephones did not help every business. Some, like the United States Postal Service, actually lost money because of telephones. People could use a phone to give information directly to a person or business without having to write and mail a letter.

Today, when you need to make a phone call, you can do it yourself. Back then, a phone call was made by picking up the phone and talking to an operator. They would connect you to the other person through a **switchboard**.

Telephones were not perfect, however. Privacy was a major concern. Anyone could pick up their receiver and listen in on other people's conversations. Early phone lines were dangerous. Workers sometimes were injured or died repairing lines. Despite this, phones had become a very important part of life.

Telephone wires could get tangled. This was dangerous for workers, who could get shocked.

A BETTER PHONE

Scientists made dramatic improvements to phones after their invention. Dr. Shirley Jackson researched the behavior of tiny particles. Because of her work, we have touch-tone telephones, caller ID, call waiting, and many other inventions.

Early telephone workers had little safety equipment to protect them.

THE PHONE GOES MOBILE

Today, people can carry their phones with them everywhere. Early phones could only be used inside a house or business. The first mobile, or cellular, phone was developed in 1946. It worked by transmitting electrical signals over radio waves rather than over telephone wires. This first mobile phone enabled a person to connect a phone inside a moving vehicle to a telephone network using radio waves. These first mobile phones were heavy and so expensive that they were mostly used by businesses and the military.

NOT WITHOUT MY PHONE!

By 2013, 87 percent of American adults and 78 percent of teenagers had cell phones. Twenty-nine percent describe their cell phone as "something they can't imagine living without."

Cooper's DynaTAC phone was one of the first popular cellular phones.

People continued inventing new phones. On April 3, 1973, inventor Martin Cooper made the first public demonstration of a handheld mobile phone. He called the Bell Labs headquarters in New Jersey from the streets of Manhattan in New York. The phone weighed about 2.5 pounds (about 1.1 kilogram) and was about 10 inches (more than 25 centimeters) long. Most mobile phones today are about 0.2 pounds (about 91 grams) and between four and five inches (10.1 and 12.7 centimeters) long.

Soon, cell phone towers were built almost everywhere. Towers raise cell phone equipment high in the air. This creates a strong cell phone signal that covers a large area. In rural places where there are not many towers, people can use **satellite** phones. These phones connect to a satellite in space to transmit messages and information.

A mountain climber uses a satellite phone.

Cell phones have changed in many ways since they were first developed.

Further advances in technology made mobile phones so small that they could fit in a pocket. Early cell phones could only make calls and, later, perform simple functions such as calculations. On December 3, 1992, the first text message was sent. That was just the beginning of the smartphone revolution that was about to come.

SMARTPHONES

Have you ever sent a text message or checked a website on a phone? If so, you were probably using a smartphone. A smartphone is a handheld personal computer that can be used to make phone calls. Smartphones can access the internet.

Instead of talking on the telephone, many people use their smartphones to communicate with text messages and social media. Smartphones can find up-to-date information instantly. Anyone can access or find information through search engines. If you have a question, you can often find the answer with just a few taps on a smartphone.

Smartphones have helped the global **economy**. People and businesses buy and sell products and services around the world using smartphones. It takes only seconds to transmit money, and there is no need for checks or cash.

A SMARTER PHONE

New phone technology is always being developed. Some phones can be used like electronic wallets. People can pay for purchases or buy subway and train tickets by putting their phone close to a special machine.

With smartphones, people can call, text, and video chat. They can pay bills, go shopping, watch a movie, or even take a class through their phone. People can communicate with someone around the world just as easily as talking to someone in the next building. Sharing information via phones has truly changed lives for the better.

PHONES AROUND THE WORLD

In 2018, it was estimated that around 4.6 billion people worldwide had mobile phones. More people have a cell phone than have a flushing toilet.

29

GLOSSARY

economy (i-KAH-nuh-mee): the system of buying, selling, and making things and managing money

networks (NET-wurkz): groups of connected devices

patent office (PAT-uhnt off-ISS): the department that registers the official invention of items

production (pruh-DUHK-shuhn): the amount produced

pulses (IM-puhls-sez): changes in intensity or beats of energy

receiver (ruh-SEE-vur): part of a telephone that turns electrical signals into sound

satellite (SAT-uh-lite): a spacecraft that is sent into orbit around something in space

switchboard (SWICH-bord): a panel used by an operator to connect telephone calls by hand

telegraphs (TEL-ih-grafs): devices for sending messages over long distances using electrical signals

transmitted (trans-MI-ted): sent or passed something from one place or person to another

INDEX

TEXT-DEPENDENT QUESTIONS

1. How did people communicate before the telephone was invented?
2. When was the first handheld mobile phone call demonstrated in public?
3. What kind of code was usually used with telegraphs?
4. How are phones related to the internet?
5. How have smartphones helped people?

EXTENSION ACTIVITY

Think of one thing that you wish a smartphone could do. Draw a simple design of a smartphone that can complete this task. Be sure to consider whether any special attachments or programs would be necessary for your plan to work.

ABOUT THE AUTHOR

There are two things Jennifer Reed loves: history and writing for kids. She thinks that understanding the past helps us do well in the future. She has written over 30 books for children and young adults. Reed lives in Vermont next to a lot of cows, which she also loves.

www.rourkeeducationalmedia.com

PHOTO CREDIT: Cover: © BogdanVj; page 1: ©Phil Lewos; pages 4-5: ©Joseph Sohm; page 6: ©JRL Photographer; pages 7, 8-9, 11, 13, 14-15, 16-17, 18a, 18-19: ©LOC; pages 9, 10: ©World History Archive; page 12: ©Everett Historical; page 16: ©MegaPixel; page 18b: ©Wiki; page 20: ©Ostill; page 21(Cooper): ©Rico Shen; page 21: ©Anna Bryukhanova; page 22: ©DMSU; page 23: ©POMPOM; pages 24-25: ©Rawpixel; page 26: ©Prykhodov; page 27: ©fizkes; page 28: ©Africa Rising; page 29a: ©DoublePhotoStudio; page 29b: ©pathdoc; page 29c: ©Radiokatka; page 29d: ©Pressmaker

Edited by: Tracie Santos
Cover and interior layout by: Kathy Walsh

Library of Congress PCN Data

Invention of Phones / Jennifer Reed
(It Changed the World)
ISBN 978-1-73162-982-1 (hard cover)(alk. paper)
ISBN 978-1-73162-977-7 (soft cover)
ISBN 978-1-73162-988-3 (e-Book)
ISBN 978-1-73163-336-1 (ePub)
Library of Congress Control Number: 2019945508

Rourke Educational Media
Printed in the United States of America,
North Mankato, Minnesota